Good News Report

Good News Report

God's Good News that Increases Our Faith

And they overcame him by the blood of the Lamb, and by the word of their testimony; and they loved not their lives unto the death.
Revelation 12:11

Prophet O´Meal O. Reid

LEGACY Publishing Services
602 N. Wymore Rd., Winter Park, FL 32789
www.LegacyPublishingServices.com

Published by:
LEGACY Publishing Services, Inc.
602 N. Wymore Road
Winter Park, Florida 32789
LegacyPublishingServices.com

Copyright © 2007 by Prophet O'Meal O. Reid
ISBN 978-1-934449-07-3
Cover design by Gabriel H. Vaughn

For comments to the author, scheduling interviews or
speaking engagements, contact :
O'Meal Reid Ministries, Inc.
P.O. Box 450039
Kissimmee, FL. 34745
407.933.1088
Email: prophetomealreid@earthlink.net

Printed in United States of America

Dedication

I would like to dedicate this book to my beautiful, God's persistent warrior wife, Pastor/Prophetess Huberta R. Reid, who is my God ordained help mate. Who's always there with me doing the work of God and my handsome son, O'Mario Wilner Reid. I also would like to dedicate this book to my only sister, Stacy Ann Reid, who I am not giving up praying for.

Last but not least, I would like to dedicate this book to all of the members of People from Every Nation Ministries, Inc. "A Place For All People" and to all of those who have received the blessings of God through my ministry.

Special Thanks

With the heart of thanksgiving, I thank my heavenly Father, my Lord and Savior Jesus Christ, and His Holy Spirit for His many blessing in my life.

Many thanks go to my Apostle, Dr. Velma Rosemond for her prayers and support. A special, special thanks to my wife who worked so hard helping me type this book.

And last, but by no means least, thanks to all of the men and women of God who have prayed and are praying for the book to be a success. I love you all. Be blessed.

Foreword

This book has been written in the right time. It is what the Body of Christ needs in this "bad news age." I'm glad you picked up this book; it's going to change your life. This book will show you the "steps" you need to know for your faith. Then on to the next step in "Breakers Anointing," and then "The Testimonies" to encourage the body of Christ. It is a must have in your library. You can share this book with a friend, family member, or a foe. I know that you will be blessed to the point you will go to your church and testify of what you were afraid of before but not now. Watch how many people will be "saved" and "delivered" through your testimony. This book will open up what is in you and it will come out to bless and edify the body of Christ.

When I read the book, I was blessed and encouraged to find out how God brought His people from test to testimonies; and from testimonies to triumph. I celebrate with them and I say, "To God Be The Glory."

Prophetess Huberta R. Reid

Table of Contents

Introduction

While driving down the road one Tuesday afternoon, my phone rang and it was one of my doctor friends. He asked how I was doing? And I replied, "I'm blessed. I have received lots of good news about all of the prophecies that were told to the people and they are witnessing the manifestation of the prophecy coming to pass in their lives. People are calling with testimonies that they have been delivered, healed, they are now in a deeper relationship with God than ever before, they have received financial breakthroughs, and so many uncommon favor blessings have been coming to pass in their lives according to the word of my prophetic voice that the Lord is using to speak." Then he said to me, "I always feel better when I get the privilege and the honor to talk to you because you always have some kind of good news about what the Lord is doing in His people lives."

To make a long story short, after I got off the phone with him, the Lord began to speak to me and said, "Prophet, son, the world is filled with bad news; every time you turn on the television, every time you turn on the radio, every time you pick up a newspaper, and nine out of ten times when people come to you, they come to you with some kind of bad news.

"You must understand that the plan of the enemy is to keep the people of God focusing on the negative instead of the positive. Nobody wants to talk about the things that I'm doing. The world is giving the devil too much acknowledgment. Its time to acknowledge the one and only Supreme Ruler of heaven and earth, the Lord Savior Jesus Christ, with some of His good news that He's doing on earth."

Prophet O'Meal O. Reid reporting live from the omnipresent spirit of God good news report.

Chapter

1

The Now Faith

The Now Faith

In this first chapter, I'm going take the time to deal with your faith in God so you can release yourself in the unlimited showers of blessings of God. I'm a living witness that your faith can purchase more than what your money can. As I was told, by one of my apostles out of Detroit Michigan, Apostle/Prophet/Dr. Velma Rosemond, "Man of God, your faith is so big. Look what the Lord is doing in such a short time; it's only because of your faith. It encourages me when I see that kind of faith you have. Your faith is big, your faith is supernatural. Words can not explain the kind of faith you have in God."

Then the Lord spoke to me and said, "Son, faith is the currency that we use to purchase anything we need out of the invisible realm of God for the manifestation of the visible realm."

Faith means faithfulness, belief, trust, with an implication that action based on that trust may follow, and assurance.

Now Faith is the substance of things hoped for, the evidence of things not seen (Hebrew 11:1 KJV).

Now Faith is the assurance (the confirmation, the title deed) of the things (we) hope for, being the proof of things (we) do not see and the conviction of their reality (faith perceiving as real what is not revealed to the sense) (Hebrew 11:1 Amplified Version).

Notice it says in the amplified version that faith perceiving as real what is not revealed to the senses. So that tells me what God is doing in your life is already done.

You are healed already.

You have the car already.

You have the house already.

You have the building already.

Your wife is pregnant already.

You have your husband already.

You have your wife already.

Your paper work is working out for you already.

You receive the contract record label deal already.

You've been noticed and found favor with great countryman and ambassadors already.

Your senses having caught up with it YET! Because your five senses are soulical, but what God is doing in your life is spiritual for the manifestation of the eternal reality.

Paul said in his epistle to the Corinthians; *"while we look not at the things which are seen, but at the things which are not seen: for the things which are seen are temporal; but the things which are not seen are eternal"* (2 Corinthians 4:18 KJV).

Apostle Paul prayed in his letter, *"[For I always pray to] the God of our Lord Jesus Christ, the Father of glory, that He may grant you a spirit of wisdom and revelation [of insight into mysteries and secrets] in the [deep and intimate] knowledge of Him"* (Ephesians 1:17 Amplified Version).

So as you can see in this passage of Scripture, we read in the amplified version, Paul was letting you know that he's interceding for you to be released on the insight of God knowing God in an intimate way.

What is the now faith? The now faith is the insight faith.

According to the Webster's Dictionary:

Insight means the ability to see and understand clearly the inner nature of things, especially by intuition. This word, intuition, goes back to be the Spirit of God that should be in operation in your life.

It is sad to admit that some of us believers don't have the now faith.

When you were born, you were born with the activation of the first Adam nature, which is in the body and the soul. The Bible said, *"And so it is written, The first man Adam was made a living soul; the last Adam was made a quickening spirit"* (1 Corinthians 15:45).

Even though the Bible said in the book of John 1:9, *"...the true light, which lighted every man that cometh in the world, you must understand that this true light does not come to activation until the heart of a man becomes convicted to repentance to be born from above."* As Jesus told Nicodemus; *"Verily, verily, I say unto thee except a man be born again, he cannot see the Kingdom of God"* (John 3:3).

Therefore, when you are born of the Spirit, you are released to operate in the insight of the now faith.

You can not have the now faith if you are not in the *last Adam nature,* which is the quickening spirit of God. *"AND YOU had He quickened, who were dead in trespasses and sin..."* (Ephesians 2:1).

The author of the book of Hebrew states that, *"But without faith it is impossible to please Him..."* (11:6 KJV).

You must understand that faith, which is the insight, is the invisible realm of God that goes back to the "king" of you being triune, which is the spirit of God. Therefore, without the insight, which is the now faith, it is impossible to please God. It was because the now faith that the men and women of God in the Bible received their breakthroughs.

The Actions of Faith

In Hebrew 11:1-3, this chapter deals with the vision and endurance of faith. It introduces us to men and women of the Old Testament who had 20/20 spiritual vision and who endured tremendous shame and suffering rather than renouncing their faith.

"By faith Sarah herself received strength to conceive seed, and was delivered of a child when she was past age, because she judged Him faithful who had promised.

"By faith Abraham, when he was tried, offered up Isaac: and he that had receive the promises offered up his only begotten son, of whom it was said, that in Isaac shall thy seed be called: accounting that God was able to raise him up, even from the dead; from whence also he received him in a figure.

"By faith Moses, when he was born, was hid three months of his parents, because they saw he was a proper child; and they were not afraid of the king's commandment.

"By faith Moses, when he was come to years, refused to be called the son of Pharaoh's daughter. Choosing rather to suffer affliction with the people of God, than to enjoy the pleasures of sin for a season" (Hebrew 11:1-3, 23-25).

The Value of Faith

Do you see what I see on the insight?

Faith is confidence in the trustworthiness of God. It is the conviction that what God says is true and what He promises will come to pass.

The Bible tells us in James' letter that, *"For as the body without the spirit is dead, so faith without works is dead"* (James 2:26 KJV).

Moreover, Apostle Paul acknowledge that, *"For by grace are ye saved through faith; and that not of yourselves: it is the gift of God"* (Ephesians 2:8 KJV).

Apostle Paul went on to encourage us by telling us that, *"Therefore being justified by faith we have peace with God through our Lord Jesus Christ"* (Romans 5:1 KJV).

All of these men and women of God wanted us to know the value of faith and how it can apply in our lives on a daily basis. I would tell you that faith is a tool that every Christian should use in order to build their confidence and their trust factor.

Now, I'm going get really radical and say something that's going make religious people uncomfortable.

You can not become a Christian without faith because it took faith to purchase your salvation. The reason why some people don't have faith is because they are not really saved. In Roman 14:23 tells us that *"...For whatsoever is not of faith is sin."*

Water baptism does not save you. It is an act of faith to know that when you immerse in water and raise up from the water that you just died with Jesus and now you are raised in Christ. In some cases, people who don't understand the meaning of water baptism can go in as a dry devil, and come out a wet devil.

Every time we get ourselves in trouble, morally or mentally, it was because we fail to see Him as He is in the lenses of faith. We have the tendency to study the problem more than the answer.

Faith is an action word. Let's pick out one out of many examples in the book of Hebrew — Noah.

"By faith Noah being warned of God of things not seen as yet, moved with fear, prepared an ark to the saving of his house; by the which he condemned the world, and became heir of the righteousness which is by faith" (Hebrew 11:7 KJV).

For Noah to believe in a God who he never saw and to build an ark to prepare for rain in a land, where it never rained before, that was faith. Not only that, but he had to wait over one hundred years for the rain to come. If you have not waited over one hundred years like Noah, then I say to you that you are disqualified to give up in your faith.

Chapter 2

The Breakers Anointing

The Breakers Anointing

In this chapter, I want to encourage you and build your faith in letting you know that you're in for a breakthrough, not a breakdown. Micah reported in his book, as the Lord inspired him; *"The breaker is come up before them: they have broken up, and have passed through the gate, and are gone out by it: and their king shall pass before them, and the LORD on the head of them"* (2:13).

In this passage of scripture, according to the principle, Micah was refering to the children of Israel in how they were being misused by the ungodly priests and how they sat up on their bed plotting evil in ways to make the children of Israel suffer. But God moved for them and gave them a breakthrough instead of a breakdown.

You are probably saying, "Prophet Reid, why is this scripture important to me right now?" Well, its important to you right now because the enemy that's been fighting you in your finance, in your children, in your marriage, in your ministry, in your walk with God, in your health, in your family relationships, in your career, and in all the promises the Lord promised you, this enemy has been defeated because of the breakers anointing.

The breaker, which literally means "one who breaks open," who is the Messiah, The King of kings; The Lord of lords; The great I AM; The beginning and the ending; Jehovah, The self existed One; The Alpha and Omega; The Lord Jesus Christ Himself. There are so many names to identify Him, but He is still the One and Only God above all gods will go before you in this season and make the crooked places straight. He will also break in pieces the gates of brass and cut in sunders the bars of iron. He will also give you the treasures of darkness and hidden riches of secret places, that you may know that He is the Lord, which call you by your name. He is the God of heaven and earth (Isaiah 42:2-3 KJV).

The breaker is the one who clears the way, removes the obstacles, and leads you through. This anointing releases you in what I call the Cyrus Anointing; *"Thus saith the LORD to his anointed, to Cyrus, whose right hand I have holden, to subdue nations before him; and I will loose the lions of kings, to open before him the two leaved gates; and the gates shall not be shut"* (Isaiah 45:1 KJV).

As you can see, the breaker's anointing cause Cyrus to break through and walk in open doors. Since God did it for Cyrus, He will do it for you. This is your season for open doors. I want you close your eyes right now and picture yourself with an army of soldiers, which are your warring angels, knocking the doors open that have been closed in your life. You must give God some praise for the open doors. The Word of the Lord said, *"...The effectual fervent prayer of the righteous man availeth much"* (James 5:16 KJV). I want to take this time to show you in scripture how to pray the Jabez curse breaker anointing prayer.

The Jabez Curse Breaker Anointing

"*And Jabez was more honorable than his brethren: and his mother called his name Jabez, saying, Because I bore him with sorrow.*

"*And Jabez called on the God of Israel, saying, Oh that thou wouldest bless me indeed, and enlarge my coast, and that thine hand might be with me, and that thou wouldest keep me from evil, that it may not grieve me! And God granted him that which he requested*" (1 Chronicles 4:9-10 KJV).

Jabez name in the Hebrew is called "ya'bes," which means to grieve. See here, according to his name, he was born in a curse already. What is the Jabez curse breaker anointing? It's a curse breaker anointing because it was after he prayed the curse broke. You must understand, my sisters and brothers, that God is no respect of person. A short, one verse prayer, with four requests, granted by God, the God of the universe can answer one prayer according to Jabez's faith and God's will married together to make a generation meaningful. Since God granted Jabez his request, surely He can and will grant your request also.

I would like to break down this prayer and reveal to you that God hears everyone who calls on His name. The first question I would ask myself when reading this passage; who is Jabez? He was a simple man, like you and me, who was respected more than his brothers; he was a religious man, living in God. He trusted God to the point he was comfortable in making those requests. I discovered when someone trust in God and has faith in Christ it is the formula that never fails in this life, nor the life to come. I am reminded of the story of Elijah. When he was ready to be "caught up" he trust in God and had faith in Christ to bring him in the next life, which we call heaven.

The first bold statement from Jabez to God is, "Oh that thou wouldest bless me indeed;" Jabez would never have considered coming to the God of Israel for a blessing without understanding something about Him. This God wants to bless His people in wealth, riches, wisdom, understanding, patience, love, joy, to have good health, and to bless his hand in every area of his life. It is alright to ask God to bless you. Some people picture God as a big white man sitting on the throne waiting for us to fall so He can use His stick to punish us. That is not how Jabez saw the God of Israel. He saw God as a giving, compassionate, and faithful God, who wants to bless His people.

The word indeed in the dictionary states; without any question or all things consider. Jabez wanted to be blessed beyond his imagination. He wanted The God of Israel to bless him more then any member of his family, any of his friends, even his foes. Don't think that word is there by accident, but it is there for us to see God has no limits in blessing us. Because he was a Jewish man, in my mind, he properly was quoting Deuteronomy 28:1-14 to assure his prayers would go up to God. When you pray God's Words back to Him, He has to move because His Word is higher then Him.

The second phrase is, "enlarge my coast/territory/borders." This prayer is the cry of becoming like his Creator. This was a bold request coming from a man that knew nothing about living big. He looked at his present circumstances and make a decision that "I am better and bigger then my circumstances. God created me to be a king in His eyes, not someone who is barely making it." For years believers have thought the less they have, the holier they are in God's eyes. I think not! Who would want to serve a

God who believes His children should be poor. We can not win the world with that mentality. Once we change our mind set and our prayers, then, we win our families, our community, and the world.

The next statement that Jabez mentioned is; "O LORD, put your hand upon me." That statement was courageous. He wanted God to bless him with His presence, His love, His power, His favor, His glory in every minute of his life. Jabez wanted God to be the center of his life. That's powerful! He knew what it meant for God's hand upon him because the history of Israel is so rich of God's promises when His hand was upon them: for example, King David. The Bible tells us that David was successful because the hand of the Lord was upon him. Jabez was asking for that kind of success, if not greater.

The fourth and final indication Jabez said is; "O LORD, keep me from evil/harm/pain/sickness/ suffering." Because his mother cursed him with his name, he asked God to brake and destroy the curse and for it not to repeat through his children or anyone else in his family. He was not only interceding for himself, but for his family. How often do you start off praying for yourself and the next thing you know you are interceding for your family, your friends, your foes, etc? It could be about personal struggles that no one knows about but you and God; for example, you can't stop smoking, you can't stop eating too much, you can't stop fornicating, you can't stop gambling, you can't stop committimg adultery on your husband or your wife, you can't stop lying, you can't stop slandering someone's name, you can't stop doing drugs, etc. The list is long, but you and God know what areas need to be worked on for your breakthrough to come to pass.

God was pleased with Jabez's prayer to the point He did not hesitate to answer him back. God granted Jabez all he requested. The Bible does not tell us in what magnitude God blessed Jabez, but I am sure Jabez died an old and prospered age. I challenge you right now to ask God to bless you indeed, and enlarge your borders, and that His hand might be with you, and that He would keep you from evil, that it might not grieve anyone else. If and when you pray that simple prayer, and believe God will hear and answer that prayer, then you will see how long God has been waiting for you to say those words to Him. Now you are going to reap the rewards of that simple prayer.

God bless you!

The Break Forth Praise

In the breakers anointing, there's one last and important thing you must know and do, which is the break forth praise. When you read the Word of God, you will notice people praised God when He moved supernaturally on their behalf and blessed them in every area of their lives.

The meaning of the word "praise" in the dictionary is to express admiration of or to honor (God) in expressing praises in words and deeds. What is the break forth praise? From my point of view, it is the unstoppable, radical thanking and honoring God praise. The kind of praise I'm talking about is the David kind of praise; *"I will praise the name of God with a song, and will magnify him with thanksgiving"* (Psalm 69:30 KJV).

David was a praiser by nature and he showed how he praised God when he was bringing the ark of God back to Jerusalem (2 Samuel 6). Instead of him wearing his royal robe, he decided to wear an ephod.

The ephod was one of eight ritual garments worn by the Israelites and later the Jewish High Priests while serving in the Jewish Temple in Jerusalem. It is sometimes translated as "apron." That means you are a servant, nothing else. David knew that two kings can not rule in one city. He lowered himself by wearing the ephod and praised the Supreme King. I can imagine, while he was dancing, leaping, praising, acting a fool like a crazy man, and acting like a child in front of the ark of the covenant, he thought of how the LORD brought him over from King Saul till then. He probably said to himself, it is the Lord's doing and it's marvelous in his eye (Psalm 118:23 KJV).

The brake forth praise is the Psalm 34:1 attitude: *"I will bless the LORD at all times: his praise shall continually be in my mouth."*

David was encouraging us in this Psalm that in spite of your circumstances you must give God a break forth praise; whether the door is shut or open, whether you have money or you are broke, whether you are sick or healed, etc. You can not let your circumstances dictate your actions in God. In giving Him the praise, the Bible said, *"sing, O barren, thou that didst not bear; break forth into singing..."* (Isaiah 54:1 KJV). Where parts of your life were barren, now God has broken forth in your life and now you can sing aloud unto Him.

The Bible clearly states, *"Let every thing that hath breath praise the LORD. Praise ye the LORD"* (Psalm 150:6 KJV). If you can inhale and exhale, then you are a candidate to praise the LORD because you were created to praise Him.

Right now I want you to take a praise break and give God some praise to release the breaker's anointing to bless you.

Chapter

3

Jehovah Rapha

Jehovah-Rapha

Jehovah-Rapha, which means "The Lord Who Heals." *"...For I, the LORD, am your healer"* (Exodus 15:26 KJV).

He is not only a healer for the physical body, but He is also a healer for the sin sick soul. Some physical or emotional illness is a consequence of personal sin. Some illnesses have other causes and some illnesses may even be for the glory of God (John 9:1-3). Whether an illness is physical, emotional, or spiritual, a person should first seek healing from Jehovah-rapha.

The key is to seek Him first. Ask Him to examine your heart before a physician ever examines your body. It is wise to have God search your heart. God always meets us at the point of our obedience, and there He comes over to our side. Jeremiah declares that only Jehovah-rapha is his healer; *"Heal me, and I will be healed; save me and I will be saved, for thou art my praise"* (Jeremiah 17:14).

The original story of Jehovah-rapha is in the Old Testament where Moses brought the Israelites to the wilderness of Shur; and they went three days in the wilderness, and found no water. When they got to Marah, they could not drink the water because it was bitter. The Israelites complained to Moses. Then Moses went to God and the LORD showed him a tree. That tree was cast in the same bitter waters and was made sweet.

The Lord wants us to know that if we be obedient to His Word, He will not put the diseases that are on the Egyptians (your enemies) on you because He is <u>your</u> God the healer.

You are properly thinking does Jehovah-rapha only exist in the Old Testament? No! He lived in the New Testament and today. I am reminded, in the Book of John, about a certain nobleman, whose son was sick at Capernaum. He heard that Jesus was going to Galilee and wanted Jesus to come to his house because his son was at the point of death. Jesus did not go to his house, but spoke six words, *"Go thy way; thy son liveth."* The man did not doubt in his heart, but believed. His servants met him half way to his house and the servants said to him, "Thy son liveth." The nobleman was curious to what time his son recovered. The servant replied, "Yesterday at the seventh hour the fever left him." That was when the nobleman remembered it was the same set hour Jesus, Jehovah-rapha, healed his son.

The point to the story is that the nobleman believed in what Jesus said. If we just believe, He will do great things for us.

The Lord does not only heal physically, but emotionally and socially. Luke tells a story that caught my attention. The story was about a woman, who was a sinner, who brought an alabaster box of ointment to Jesus. She was a woman who society put away because the kind of life she chose. Jesus, who knows the heart of man, heard what Simon the Pharisee said to himself, "if He is a prophet, He would know what manner of woman this was." Jesus told him a story about two debtors; one who owed five hundred pence and the other fifty. To make a long story short, they could not pay back what they owed, so the borrower forgave them both. Jesus asked Simon which of them will love him most? The one who owed more; Jesus replied, you answer correct. Then He reproached Simon and said, *"I entered into thine house, thou gavest me no water for my feet: but she hath washed my feet with tears, and wiped them with the hairs of her head.*

"Thou gavest me no kiss: but this woman since the time I came in, hath not ceased to kiss my feet. My head with oil thou didst not anoint: but this woman hath anointed my feet with ointment. She was forgiven of her sins, which were many" (Luke 7:44 – 46). This woman received Jehovah-rapha's special healing in another way.

She experienced unspeakable joy for the first time, peace like never before for the first time, love without giving up anything for the first time. This is what Jehovah-rapha did for her. He not only healed Mary Magdalene emotionally and sociably, but He made her whole. After that day, she'd never be the same. In fact, she was the one who told the disciples that Jesus Christ was raised from the dead. So many of us are like this woman. If you seek after Him and kiss His presence, He will testify on your behalf, and for your reward, you also will go home refreshed, revived, and renewed.

There are so many different stories in the Bible that talk about the wonderful healing touch of our Jehovah-rapha, but I chose the original story and two stories in the New Testament because that's how you know that He's not a respect of person, but He is a respect of principles. You can be obedient to God; whether you are Jew or gentile, rich or poor, educated or ignorant. The principles of God are for everyone. If you just trust Him, you will see how God will work in your life. So, if you are in distress? Troubled? Weary? Wondering how you're going to make it through the day? Run into the strong tower of His healing name. Only He can take your bitterness and make it sweet, turn your mourning into dancing, make beauty for ashes.

We have a reason to celebrate Jehovah-rapha, for all He's done for us and what He will continue to do in our future.

Praise the LORD!

Chapter

4

Testimonies

Testimonies

"And they overcame him by the blood of the Lamb, and by the word of their testimony; and they loved not their lives unto the death" (Revelation 12:11).

Renew your mind with these testimonies.

In this chapter, you will read about different types of testimonies of what the Lord has done through my ministry, of Him using me and my wife Pastor/Prophetess Huberta R. Reid. I give <u>ALL</u> the glory to God.

First, I would like to point your attention to a young man of God, Minister Quincy and his wife Margaret. In the midst of the Lord using me and my wife to teach on firstfruit in our church, People From Every Nation Ministries, Inc., "A Place For All People" located in Kissimmee, Florida, which is a five-fold ministry operating strongly in the prophetic anointing of God.

Minister Quincy and Margaret gave their first check in the beginning of the year as their firstfruit offering to the ministry. Since then they had been physically and financially blessed.

The first blessing is the physical; Margaret had a bleeding disorder and God used me to lay hands and agree that she would be healed and she's been healed ever since and they thank God for this miracle. Notice I said a miracle and not just a healing because often times when a wound has been healed, it leaves a scar.

However, in this case, she has been totally healed and there's no symptom of this disease anymore.

The second is financial; they are now the proud owners of a five-bedroom and four-bathroom home.

Plus, Margaret is the owner of her own daycare. This is just the beginning of the great things God is doing in their lives since joining the ministry. Tell the Lord Thank You!

Have you ever felt like there's no more purpose in living? If so, I want to let you know there are many people all around the world that, after suffering so many afflictions, they are ready to give up. But, I want to encourage you in what David said in the book of Psalm, *"Many are the affliction of the righteous: but the LORD delivereth him out of them all"* (34:19).

Cathy was one victim in this testimony that was ready to give up. Suffering with depression and wanting to die. She felt her spirit was melting away. But in her visitation at the ministry, the Lord used me to call her forward and denounced the death angel off of her life. My wife, Pastor/Prophetess Reid, saw her bad heart problem and prayed for God to restore her heart like it was before. Since that day, she has confessed that she is a new person in her body and her spirit. She promised the Lord that she will serve Him until she goes home to be with Him, but for right now, as she always says, "I'm alive and kick'in." God is Good!

Now we have here sister Laressa who visited the ministry for the first time. The Lord used me tell her about her stomach condition, that she is going to be healed. To her amazement, she has not had any issue with her stomach since that day. The second time she visited the ministry, I called her up again, in front of the church, and told her that her finances and life will improve. I continued to say that her husband will change his ways and join this ministry. At first, she found it too good to be true, but after she sowed a sacrificial seed of one thousand dollars towards the church building fund, shortly after, her husband came to church and the Lord used me to speak into his life.

Her husband, Peter, accepted Jesus as his Savior and Lord on that day. Since that day, Peter was blessed to purchase his own 18-wheeler and now owns his trucking company. He blessed his wife, Laressa, with a new Excursion Truck. Shortly after purchasing the truck, her husband blessed her again with a PT Cruiser, which she uses for work and everyday use. God deserve the glory!

Minister Annette H. Southward, who is now a member of the ministry, on the first occasion of me meeting her the Lord used me to prophesize to her that God has an evangelistic calling on her life and even though she is mature in age, it is not too late to walk fully in that calling. Since she joined the ministry, she has been blessed spiritually and financially. In the spiritual aspect, she counted it a privilege to walk with people who fear God and she explains that she has been blessed by Prophet and Prophetess Reid's teaching on the prophetic.

In the financial part, she planted a seed of one hundred dollars in the ministry towards her business so it can expand. The following year, she had to hire more staff to her business, which is a bookkeeping and accounting firm. Also, she was blessed to receive unexpected checks in the mail. God is Awesome!

Mother McInotch, in the first five months of her joining the ministry, she experienced a spiritual growth like never before. She was baptized in the Holy Ghost with the evidence of speaking with heavenly tongues. She has not been the same since. Now, she is telling everyone about this ministry and reaching souls wherever she goes; in the bank, in the grocery store, and the hair salon. It was a joy for her to see her son received Jesus as his Lord and Savior, and now he is a business man in New York. God is Good!

Erma testified that it was her first time hearing about firstfruit. She obeyed the voice of the Lord and she did the firstfruit. As a result of her obedience, she was healed from diabetes and she received three unexpected checks in the mail. Thank You, Jesus!

My wife and I were visiting a local church when I saw Sister Muriel and the Lord told me to call her out.

After that manner, the Lord used me to dismantle the generation bloodline curses off of her life and I denounced cancer and diabetes. After she came back from her doctor's appointment, the tests came back negative. The Lord used me to continue to say that her children are going to be blessed. To her children's surprise, they now have their own houses, cars, and businesses. Last but not least, her spiritual life has grown so much and she is grateful to God allowing Him to use us for her. Bless the Lord!

Does a woman have the right to divorce her husband because of impotency? Well, in this case, this man of God that I am going to tell you a little about was truly broken after he found out that his wife is divorcing him because he can not please her. I want to introduce you to Evangelist John from Africa. John testifies that he was suffering from an impotence sickness that caused him to lose his marriage. He testified that after the Lord used me to lay hands on him for healing and called out his sickness and prayed over a bottle of water and told him to drink it. A month later, he was totally healed. This was truly a miracle of God. Oh, give the Lord praise. Take this time to give the Lord praise. Thank You, Lord for being the lifter of my head!

Are you waiting for a divine miracle that you heard people talk about so many times? Well, one of my sisters in the Lord is one. She was in one of the services that I preached. At the end of my alter call, I looked at her and said, "What are you doing in that wheelchair? The Lord showed me you three weeks before I came here and He told me to tell you to get up and walk." She replied to me, "I was born this way, I have the disease of weak muscles and my muscles are not strong enough for me to stand up and walk." This sister, who was in her twenties, doubting in her mind thinking, "I can not do this, I've been like this all my life."

Everybody was around me watching to see what was going to happen. Then I prayed the first time, nothing happened. I scratched my head and said Lord I know what you showed me. Then I prayed the second time, nothing happened. At that time, the devil spoke to me and said, "You are making a fool of yourself." I rebuke the devil's voice immediately. Then I said, "If there is anybody in this room who doesn't believe that she can get out of the wheelchair and walk, you can leave." I prayed the third time and finally she got out of the wheelchair and stood up, and now I commanded her to walk. She walked around the church three times and then she began to run and scream, saying, "I can walk! I can walk!" The congregation was amazed by holding their heads and praising God with a loud shout. At the end of the service, she pushed the wheelchair out herself instead of someone pushing her. This sister is still walking and now is married and gave birth to four beautiful children. Give God Praise!

Mary, who was twenty-five years old at the time, found out that she had HIV. The doctors gave her thirty days to live. She called me for prayer, explaining to me that she was in need for a healing.

However, she was not being specific of what she needed from the Lord, through prayer, because she was ashamed. As I began to pray, the Holy Spirit revealed to me that she had HIV.

I told her what the Lord said and she began to cry and asked how did you know? I replied that the Lord revealed it to me. She explained to me that she was unable to defecate for three months and her stomach was about to bust. She continued to say that she lost a lot of blood and began to look pale. I told her to get a glass of water and put her hand over it. Then I began to pray. In the middle of my prayer, the Holy Spirit told me to tell her to drink the water and then go sit on the toilet. When she sat on the toilet, her bowels began to move and the toilet was filled with maggots. She had to rush and flush the toilet. After that, the Lord said that she is healed from HIV. She began to cry and praise God. When she went to the doctor, they told her that she is AIDS FREE! Hallelujah!

Are you suffering with a sickness called cancer? If yes, right now this is a perfect opportunity for God to heal you. I want to first build your faith by telling you about a man of God who is one of my fathers in the Lord. He was diagnosed with prostate cancer, which was a threat to shorten his life. At that time, the Lord gave me an assignment to intercede at his church one day out of the week. One night of being there, interceding for that ministry and God's people in general all around the nations, the glory of the Lord came and filled the house. As I began to speak in my heavenly language, the Spirit of the Lord told me to lay my hands on him and told him when he goes back to the doctor they will find no sign of cancer in his body. Shortly after going to the doctor, he brought the report to show that he was totally healed from prostate cancer. Tell God Thank You!

I will not forget a woman by the name of Berta. I met her through a mutual friend over the phone. In the midst of the conversation, I started praying and started speaking over her life. I described how she looked, what church she went to, and the husband she is supposed to marry. She did not say too much when I was speaking; however, she did acknowledge that all I had said was correct. The following night, she and the mutual friend called me again, but this time she was in better spirits. She started laughing and opening up more to me and she wanted to thank me for allowing God to use me for her.

I thought nothing of it, but four days later I received a package in the mail. She had planted a seed and expressed her gratitude towards the prophet of the Lord. Shortly after, we started speaking on a daily basis and I introduced her to worship.

The Lord started using me to develop what was in her, and what she was doing in her local church was not what God intended for her to do for the rest of her life. The relationship grew and she became my armor bearer. We traveled from state to state, from city to city. She loved what God was doing in her life. She found meaning in her living again. If you are one of those persons who thought "because my grandmother, grandfather, mom, and dad were in this church for such a long time I can not leave," God is letting you know that your season is up. Ask the Lord to order your steps in the right church where He will plant you and you will blossom. Berta has not been the same. She is now a prophetess and speaking life to those persons whose spirit is dead. Since God did it for Berta, then surely He can do it for you. Glory to His name!

Chapter 5

Sowers are Reapers

Sowers are Reapers

God has told us clearly that in order for us to reap a harvest, we must sow a seed. If you take God at His Word, you will be living under open windows at all times and you will show the world how a child of God should live on earth. You will show the world that there is heaven on earth. It is your time to experience God's supernatural increase and abundance for your life in this year.

The Lord said there's been a spirit of poverty over the lives of the believers because of the lack of giving. However, today is your day to be free from it because He sent me as a prophet to free you out of it. I am a living witness that when you give to the Kingdom of God, you put a demand on the wealth of the KING to give back to you. I know you are saying, "Prophet, can you show me that in the Bible, *'Give and it shall be given unto you; good measure, pressed down, and shaken together, and running over, shall men give into your bosom'* (Luke 6:38)."

Jesus doesn't specify what is to be given (sown). However, he does promise that whatever we give, we shall receive it back again, but in more abundantly.

The Law of Sowing and Reaping

According to the Epistle of the Apostle Paul to the Galatians, he was telling the Galatians about the law of reciprocity.

"Be not deceived; God is not mocked: for whatsoever a man soweth, that shall he also reap" (Galatians 6:7). We often hear this particular verse quote out of context and make us think it only goes one way. The soweth in the Greek means sow seed or scatter seeds. The word seed by itself means a lot.

It could mean your money, your words, and your deeds. Whatsoever you and I will do, there will be a "reward" in it for us. We cannot trick God into thinking that we always do the right thing, but we can show Him that we are trying to spread good seed everywhere we go.

"For he that soweth to his flesh shall of the flesh reap corruption; but he that soweth to the Spirit shall of the Spirit shall of the Spirit reap life everlasting." We must be aware how we treat our bodies: rather in food, sex, or anything else. God wants us to live in a way the world would want to mimic us in order to win them to Christ.

"And let us not be weary in well doing: for in due season we shall reap, if we faint not; there is a set time God is going to get glory out of our lives if we faint not" (Galatians 6:8-10). I can understand that you have been sowing and you feel that your harvest is not coming fast enough or is dead, but the Word says FAINT NOT! You can not give up now. You put so much out for you to turn back. I am encouraging you right now my friend, my colleague, my suffering brother and sister in the gospel, for the love of God, please don't give up.

The Bible is full of God's promises and you can take Him at His Word because He is God. He can not lie. That is not in his character. What He says with His mouth, He will do with His arms in due season. The Apostle Paul was showing the Corinthian church that if you sow sparingly, you shall reap also sparingly; and if you sow bountifully, you shall reap bountifully (2 Corinthians 9:6).

There are two words in this verse I would like for you to get an understanding in knowing the difference between sparingly and bountiful harvest. Sparingly means to hold in, reserve, not liberal.

That definition means God is limited in what He can give you. However, the word bountiful means given freely and plentiful. This definition is what I want for my life on a daily basis, and, so, I practice it every time I get the chance. God only rewards those who obey His Word. If we want a mediocre harvest, then sow sparingly. However, if you are looking for a supernatural harvest that your grandchildren will inherit and enjoy, then you need to start practicing the bountiful given. If you take the limits off of God, He will show you He wants to bless you beyond your capacity.

Apostle Paul continued to stress the importance of giving in the same chapter, *"God is able to make all grace abound toward you; that ye, always having all sufficiency in all things, may abound to every good work"* (2 Corinthians 9:8). The phrase "God is able" is to supply us with resources so that we will not only have a sufficiency ourselves, but so that we will be able to share what we have with others and thus have abundance for every good work.

The word "all" in the Greek means all. When you have all, there is nothing left. That is where God wants us to be having it ALL. It only starts by you and I doing our part and He will do His. God will not do what we can do and we can't do what He can do. Let me share something with you; God doesn't need or want your money, He wants to see if you can take Him at His Word and act on it!

Living Under Open Windows

I want to point your attention to Deuteronomy 28:12 which shows you the blessing of your obedience to the word of God, *"The LORD shall open unto thee his good treasure, the heaven to give the rain unto thy land in his season, and to bless all the work of thine hand: and thou shalt lend unto many nations, and thou shalt not borrow."*

Open, *in the Hebrew* =
   to loosen,
   to release,
   to take off,
   to set wide,
   to set forth,
   to drawn out,
   to spread out
   to open wide,
   to break forth,
   to free oneself,
   to be unstoppable.

Good, *in the Hebrew* =
   well,
   best,
   merry,
   wealth,
   precious,
   pleasing,
   prosperity,
   any thing that is better.

Treasure, *in the Hebrew* = storehouse.

Heaven is the invisible realm of God. Notice the definition says the invisible realm of God; this heaven is refering to the heaven of heavens. It is the third heaven, which is the invisible realm of God.

There's a woman in the Bible who showed how heaven will open when she sowed into the man of God. This woman is found in 1 Kings 17:8- 24.

The Lord had commanded this woman to sustain the man of God (Elijah). She was going to collect some sticks together and make her and her son a piece of bread to eat and wait to die. The man of God intervenes on her pity party and demands a strange request. Elijah said, "Make me a little cake first," then her and her son. The heaven opened up for this woman when she obeyed the command of the man of God. You're probably asking yourself what was her reward? *"Her barrel of meal wasted not, neither did the cruse of oil fail, according to the word of the LORD, which he spake by Elijah"* (verse 16).

Unfortunately, tragedy hit her house shortly after she gained her harvest. Her son fell sick and later died. Elijah took the young boy to his loft and prayed for him to come back from the dead. The Lord heard the voice of Elijah and granted him his request. The boy revived and the man of God brought back the young boy back to his mother. It was after the fact she confessed to him, *"Now by this I know that thou art a man of God, and that the word of the LORD in thy mouth is true"* (verse 24).

Your harvest can turn from one thing to another, like this woman. You may think when you sow, you are suppose to reap right away. Not in all cases. Your harvest will come in at the right time of your life. Her harvest was in two-fold miracles. The first one was in the barrel of meal and the cruse of oil. The second miracle was when her son was revived by Elijah. Likewise for us, we need to know when we sow in a man or woman of God, we are going to reap some unexpected blessing. So, get ready for an unexpected harvest!

Remember, Sowers are reapers!

I'm ready to give NOW to release my harvest!

Chapter 6

Prayer Of Salvation

Prayer Of Salvation

If you are not sure that you are saved and would like to experience salvation in Christ, please say the following prayer from your heart:

Dear Father, please forgive me and cleanse me from all my sin. I accept and receive Jesus Christ today as my Savior and my Lord. Fill me with Your Holy Spirit. Thank you for your mercy and grace toward me, amen.

Congratulations on your decision for Christ, please write to me and let me hear your testimony.

O'Meal Reid Ministries, Inc.
P.O. Box 450039
Kissimmee, FL. 34745
407.933.1088
Email: prophetomealreid@earthlink.net

About the Author

Prophet Reid is an ambitious and motivated soul's winner for the kingdom of God. Prophet Reid is called, commissioned, and ordained by God to speak to nations and operates through the prophetic anointing and has the manifestation of the revelation gifts of prophecy. Prophet Reid is the senior pastor and founder of People From Every Nation Ministries in Kissimmee, Florida and he is the founder and president of O'Meal Reid Ministries.

The Lord has allowed him to travel throughout Florida and abroad evangelizing, singing, teaching, and preaching the Word of God. He has been baptized and Holy Ghost filled with a vision to carry the gospel all over the world and is winning souls for Christ. In his years of evangelizing through the powerful anointing of God that is upon his life people are receiving miracles and healing from cancer, AIDS, crippliness and all other manner of sickness.

God has anointed Prophet Reid with yokes destroying anointing that leads people into the "Open Glory of God" to bring forth restoration, deliverance, salvation, and cause the abundant blessing of God to come into their lives. Prophet Reid is also the proud husband of the beautiful Prophetess Huberta R. Reid and the proud father of O'Mario Wilner Reid.

Prophet Reid is like Samuel in the Scripture; his word hasn't fallen to the ground.

Prophet Reid is available for speaking engagements. conference, revival, and prophetic workshops.